# 101
# Knock Knock
# Jokes for Kids

I.P. Grinning
&
I.P. Factly

# DEDICATION

To Jacob & Riley.

## 1.

Knock Knock!

Who's there?

Randy.

Randy who?

Randy last three miles - I need a lie down!

## 2.

Knock Knock!

Who's there?

Letters.

Letters who?

Letters in and you'll find out!

**3.**

Knock Knock!

Who's there?

Turner.

Turner who?

Turner your music down!

**4.**

Knock Knock!

Who's there?

Ice cream.

Ice cream who?

Ice cream every time I see your face!

## 5.

Knock!

Who's there?

Eileen.

Eileen who?

Eileen down bang my head on your door and you ask "who's there?"

## 6.

Knock Knock!

Who's there?

Isabelle.

Isabelle who?

Isabelle not needed on your door?

## 7.

Knock Knock!

Who's there?

Underwear.

Underwear who?

I underwear the key is?

## 8.

Knock Knock!

Who's there?

Ben.

Ben who?

Ben wondering if you'd let me in?

## 9.

Knock Knock!

Who's there?

Ben.

Ben who?

Ben knocking on your door all morning!

## 10.

Knock Knock!

Who's there?

Doris.

Doris who?

Doris stuck – let me in!

## 11.

Knock Knock!

Who's there?

Anita.

Anita who?

Anita use the bathroom!

## 12.

Knock Knock!

Who's there?

Aida.

Aida who?

Aida pint of water and now I'm desperate!

## 13.

Knock Knock!

Who's there?

Lisa.

Lisa who?

Lisa you can do is let me use your bathroom!

## 14.

Knock Knock!

Who's there?

Butter.

Butter who?

Butter let me in, I'm desperate!

## 15.

Knock Knock!

Who's there?

Tank.

Tank who?

You're welcome!

## 16.

Knock Knock!

Who's there?

Isabelle.

Isabelle who?

Isabelle not working?

## 17.

Knock Knock!

Who's there?

Ali.

Ali who?

Ali tull old man who can't reach the doorbell!

## 18.

Knock Knock!

Who's there?

I could.

I could who?

I could reach the doorbell, but I shrank!

## 19.

Knock Knock!

Who's there?

Goose.

Goose who!

Goose who's knocking at your door?

## 20.

Knock Knock!

Who's there?

Luke.

Luke who?

Luke through the window and find out!

## 21.

Knock Knock!

Who's there?

Spider.

Spider who?

Spider through the keyhole!

## 22.

Knock Knock!

Who's there?

Wood.

Wood who?

Wood you let me in? It's freezing!

## 23.

Knock Knock!

Who's there?

Arch.

Arch who?

Bless You!

## 24.

Knock Knock!

Who's there?

Atish.

Atish who?

Are you catching a cold?

## 25.

Knock Knock!

Who's there?

Eddie.

Eddie who?

Eddie idea how to cure this cold!

## 26.

Knock Knock!

Who's there?

Hannah.

Hannah who?

Hannah me that screwdriver and I'll fix your doorbell!

## 27.

Knock Knock!

Who's there?

Colin.

Colin who?

Colin to see how you are!

## 28.

Knock Knock!

Who's there?

Cargo.

Cargo who?

No! Cargo "brum! brum!"

## 29.

Knock Knock!

Who's there?

Margo.

Margo who?

No! Margo "Tidy Your Room!"

## 30.

Knock Knock!

Who's there?

Cowgo.

Cowgo who?

No! Cowgo "Moo!"

## 31.

Knock Knock!

Who's there?

Moo.

Moo who?

Aah... Don't cry little cow!

## 32.

Knock Knock!

Who's there?

Madam.

Madam who?

Madam foot is stuck in the door!

## 33.

Knock Knock!

Who's there?

Olivia.

Olivia who?

Olivia, so get out my house!

## 34.

Knock Knock!

Who's there?

Water.

Water who?

Water you deaf of something?

## 35.

Knock Knock!

Who's there?

Lemonade.

Lemonade who?

Lemonade you in the purchase of a door-bell!

## 36.

Knock Knock!

Who's there?

Phillip.

Phillip who?

Phillip the gas tank, I'm almost out!

## 37.

Knock Knock!

Who's there?

Denis.

Denis who?

Denis says I need a tooth out!

## 38.

Knock Knock!

Who's there?

Bee.

Bee who?

Bee a dear and let me in!

## 39.

Knock Knock!

Who's there?

Ben.

Ben who?

Ben dover so I can kick you in the rear!

## 40.

Knock Knock!

Who's there?

Neil.

Neil who?

Neil down you're making me feel small!

## 41.

Knock Knock!

Who's there?

Watson.

Watson who?

What's on TV?

## 42.

Knock Knock

Who's there?

Cook.

Cook who?

Hey! Who are you calling cuckoo?

## 43.

Knock Knock!

Who's there?

Dishes.

Dishes who?

Dishes your friend, please let me in!

## 44.

Knock Knock!

Who's there?

Dishes.

Dishes who?

Dishes a nice doorstep, but let me in!

**45.**

Knock Knock!

Who's there?

Dishes.

Dishes who?

Dishes getting boring now! LET ME IN!

**46.**

Knock Knock!

Who's there?

Pickle.

Pickle who?

Pickle little flower for your momma!

## 47.

Knock Knock!

Who's there?

Jess.

Jess who?

Jess calling to see how you are!

## 48.

Knock Knock!

Who's there?

Les.

Les who?

Les go see a movie!

## 49.

Knock Knock!

Who's there?

Vaughan.

Vaughan who?

Vaughan day you'll buy a new doorbell!

## 50.

Knock Knock!

Who's there?

Fanny.

Fanny who?

Fanny body calls, I'm on your doorstep!

## 51.

Knock Knock!

Who's there?

Fanny.

Fanny who?

Fanny body going to let me in?

## 52.

Knock Knock!

Who's there?

Fanny.

Fanny who?

Fanny you keep saying "who's there?" but never let me in!

## 53.

Knock Knock!

Who's there?

Safari.

Safari who?

Safari so good with the knock knock jokes!

## 54.

Knock Knock!

Who's there?

Aardvark.

Aardvark who?

Aardvark forward and open this door if I were you!

## 55.

Knock Knock!

Who's there?

Ivan.

Ivan who?

Ivan a new coat, do you like it?

## 56.

Knock Knock!

Who's there?

Ya.

Ya who?

What are you getting so excited about?

## 57.

Knock Knock!

Who's there?

Woo.

Woo who?

Stop getting so excited! They're only knock knock jokes!

## 58.

Knock Knock!

Who's there?

Wendy.

Wendy who?

Wendy going to let me in?

## 59.

Knock Knock!

Who's there?

Justin.

Justin who?

Justin time for lunch!

## 60.

Knock Knock!

Who's there?

Lee.

Lee who?

Lee me alone I'm tired!

## 61.

Knock Knock!

Who's there?

Police.

Police who?

Police help me stop telling knock knock jokes!

## 62.

Knock Knock!

Who's there?

Bet.

Bet who?

Bet you don't know who's at the door!

## 63.

Knock Knock!

Who's there?

Hugh.

Hugh who?

Hugh won't believe your eyes!

## 64.

Knock Knock!

Who's there?

Sabina.

Sabina who?

Sabina long time since I've seen you!

## 65.

Knock Knock!

Who's there?

Lass.

Lass who?

Lass time I saw you was 2 years ago!

## 66.

Knock Knock!

Who's there?

Pierre.

Pierre who?

Pierre through the keyhole to see me!

## 67.

Knock Knock!

Who's there?

Sam.

Sam who?

Sam day you'll remember me!

## 68.

Knock Knock!

Who's there?

Dwayne.

Dwayne who?

Dwayne the bathtub, I'm dwowning!

## 69.

Knock Knock!

Who's there?

Nana.

Nana who?

Nana your business!

## 70.

Knock Knock!

Who's there?

Waiter.

Waiter who?

Waiter right there, I've got more doors to knock on!

## 71.

Knock Knock!

Who's there?

Zany.

Zany who?

Zany body in?

## 72.

Knock Knock!

Who's there?

Ida.

Ida who?

Ida epic journey getting here!

## 73.

Knock Knock!

Who's there?

Comb.

Comb who?

Comb on open the door!

## 74.

Knock Knock!

Who's there?

Despair.

Despair who?

Despair tire was flat, can I use your phone?

## 75.

Knock Knock!

Who's there?

Nobel.

Nobel who?

Nobel, that's why I knocked!

## 76.

Knock Knock!

Who's there?

Unite.

Unite who?

Unite a person, and then you call him Sir!

## 77.

Knock Knock!

Who's there?

Howl.

Howl who?

Howl you know unless you open the door!

## 78.

Knock Knock!

Who's there?

Scott.

Scott who?

Scott nothing to do with you!

## 79.

Knock Knock!

Who's there?

Disguise.

Disguise who?

Disguise after me! Let me in!

## 80.

Knock Knock!

Who's there?

Ken.

Ken who?

Ken I come in, it's raining?

## 81.

Knock Knock!

Who's there?

Formosa.

Formosa who?

Formosa the summer I was on holiday!

## 82.

Knock Knock!

Who's there?

Island.

Island who?

Island on your roof with my parachute!

## 83.

Knock Knock!

Who's there?

Dakota.

Dakota who?

Dakota has no hood and it's raining!

## 84.

Knock Knock!

Who's there?

Radio.

Radio who?

Radio not, here I come!

## 85.

Knock Knock!

Who's there?

Juno.

Juno who?

Juno your door is locked!

## 86.

Knock Knock!

Who's there?

Seymour.

Seymour who?

Seymour if you open the door!

## 87.

Knock Knock!

Who's there?

Viper.

Viper who?

Viper your nose - it's running!

## 88.

Knock Knock!

Who's there?

Howie.

Howie, who?

Howie bout opening the door!

## 89.

Knock Knock!

Who's there?

Owl.

Owl who?

Owl be sad if you don't let me in!

## 90.

Knock Knock!

Who's there?

Baby owl.

Baby owl who?

Baby owl see you later, maybe I won't!

## 91.

Knock Knock!

Who's there?

Twitter.

Twitter who?

It's that baby owl again!

## 92.

Knock Knock!

Who's there?

Who.

Who who ?

Will all the owls please leave -NOW!

## 93.

Knock Knock!

Who's there?

Ammonia.

Ammonia who?

Ammonia going to ask you once!

## 94.

Knock Knock!

Who's there?

Henrietta.

Henrietta who?

Henrietta worm in an apple!

## 95.

Knock Knock!

Who's there?

Betty.

Betty who?

Betty wishes he had a coat like this!

## 96.

Knock Knock!

Who's there?

Imogen.

Imogen who?

Imogen life with a doorbell!

## 97.

Knock Knock!

Who's there?

Finders.

Finders who?

Finders my keys, I can't get in!

## 98.

Knock Knock!

Who's there?

Chicken.

Chicken who?

Chicken your pockets - I think you might have my keys!

## 99.

Knock Knock!

Who's there?

Donut!

Donut who?

Donut look now but there's a lion behind you!

## 100.

Knock Knock!

Who's there?

Lionel.

Lionel who?

Lionel eat you if you come in!

## 101.

Knock Knock!

Who's there?

Candice.

Candice who?

Candice be the last Knock Knock joke please?

# ABOUT THE AUTHOR

IP Factly is the happy father of 7 and 9 year old boys. Their hilariously awful attempts to make up their own jokes inspired the IP Factly series of joke books for kids.

IP Factly has previously written questions for the UK's 'Who Wants to be a Millionaire' quiz machine and loves questions as much as he loves answers.

Hopefully you'll enjoy this book as much as he enjoyed writing it.

Made in the USA
Middletown, DE
08 June 2015